I0168483

The
LITTLE RED BOOK
OF WORDPLAY:
—WITH *PERSPICACIOUS* THE CAT

LELAND JAMES

ILLUSTRATED BY:
ANNE ZIMANSKI

FIRST EDITION

Little Red Tree Publishing, LLC,
509 W 3rd Street, North Platte, NE 69101

Little Red Tree Publishing
Previous books by Leland James

Animal Land, An Allegorical Fable (2015)

Longberry's Leap (2017)

A Mice Christmas: —At Valerie's Place (2017)

Layout and Cover Design: Michael Linnard
Text in Minion Pro, Trajan Pro and Ariel.

First Edition, 2018, manufactured in USA
1 2 3 4 5 6 7 8 9 10 LSI 24 23 22 21 20 19 18

All illustrations in this book are by Anne Zimanski. Her photo on page 77 was taken by Danielle Nowicki, and is reproduced here by kind permission.

Leland James photograph, on page 79 and back cover, was taken by John Robert Williams and is reproduced here by kind permission.

Library of Congress Cataloging-in-Publication Data

Names: James, Leland., author.
Title: The Little Red Book of Wordplay: —With *Perspicacious* the Cat/ by Leland James
Description: First edition. | North Platte, NE : Little Red Tree
  Publishing, 2018.
Identifiers: LCCN 2018156398 | ISBN 9781935656586 (pbk. : alk. paper)
Subjects: LCSH: Children's Poetry/Words
Classification: LCC PS3573.I5987 A6 2018 | DDC 811/.6--dc23

Little Red Tree Publishing LLC
509 W 3rd Street,
North Platte, NE 69101
www.littleredtree.com

I would like to thank Michael Linnard at Little Red Tree publishing for his continuing support, Betty Carlton for her eagle-eye proofing, and my wife Anndy, always my first reader and advisor. Also, the Kundmueller and Berg children who served as "guinea pigs" on the several drafts of the book.

CONTENTS

AUTHOR'S NOTE

Author's Note to Parents, Teachers,
and Other Adult Mentors:
How to use this book

The Little Red Book of Wordplay is for kids, and their helping adults. The age range is 9-12, but of course that can vary widely with the individual young person. The book is either an introduction to literary devices or a hands-on review and practice. It is not meant as a comprehensive text for the target age level. The takeaway is intended to be a feel for and the fun of words. The main definitions are provided in each lesson, and it is fine to know them. But it is much more important, I think, for young learners to have a feel for literary devices and begin to use them, to recognize their magic and see them not as academic exercises but as a source of enjoyment and enlightenment.

Most young learners will require an adult to aid them in navigating the materials. There is in my view a tendency in education to confuse immediate gratification (easy) with the deeper gratification of learning and the joy of accomplishment. *Perspicacious*, for instance, is not an easy word to pronounce. Many learners will not master it until the latter lessons. Most will at this latter point (the book has been extensively tested with 9-12 year olds) enjoy the *taste* of the word and, with a little prompting, appreciate why *Perspicacious the Cat* is so named. He is a personification, one of the lessons. Similarly, tongue twisters in the first lesson are not merely an entertaining pastime. Tongue twisters foster articulation and careful reading, as well as being fun. In the final analysis, mastery and enjoyment go hand in hand.

The book is divided into thirteen lessons. It teaches the literary devices you'll find in the table of contents. The "Perspicacious Challenge," included with each lesson, encourages *wordplay*. Each lesson is built on several levels. Examples and challenges contain a range of difficulty to stretch the more advanced learners. Adults can productively step in to help if the stretch is too far. Similarly, adult mentors will find, along with obvious wordplays aimed at young learners, more sophisticated wordplays and hidden examples that many young learners may miss. These may be pointed out by adult mentors, increasing interaction and enhancing each lesson. Vocabulary words are established, along with a brief definition, at the outset of each lesson. This sets the stage for expansion in verse, more detailed definition, examples, and wordplay in the form of the challenges. The number of vocabulary words may at first seem daunting. But in testing the materials it was found that most learners already know or have some sense of a portion of the vocabulary words. Reinforcement of more sophisticated and difficult to pronounce words, as well as acquisition, is intended. The verses that accompany each lesson may be productively read aloud by the adult before the young learners attempt the meter and meaning themselves. More than one repetition will often be beneficial to achieve both comprehension and rhythm. Verse, by its nature, demands the articulate and careful reading that is frequently wanting in early readers—they skip words, misread and mispronounce. Careful reading of the verses aloud can be fun and instructive. The remainder of each lesson is best gone over interactively. The challenges can be either joint adventures or "homework" as best fits the individual case.

Wordplay, beyond its joy and intellectual benefits, along with basic grammar and syntax, is the gateway to creative writing. W. H. Auden, three times nominated for the Nobel Prize in Literature, was once asked what advice he would give to a young person who wished to become a poet. His reply pertains, I believe, to creative writing in general. Auden replied that he would ask the young person why he or she wanted to write poetry. If the answer was 'because I have something important to say,' Auden would conclude that there was no hope for the young person as a poet. If on the other hand the answer was something like 'because I like to hang around words and overhear them talking to one another,' then that young person was at least interested in a fundamental part of the poetic process and there was hope for him or her. So for those learners with a creative writing bent, the lessons may be a gateway to creative writing in general.

A final point: Figurative language, at its most basic, is perhaps far more important in the educational process than is typically perceived. Consider this, from famed poet, former Poet Laureate of the USA, Robert Frost: "[U]nless you are at home in the metaphor, unless you had proper poetical education in metaphor, you are not safe anywhere. Because you are not at ease with figurative values: you don't know the metaphor in its strength and its weakness…. You are not safe in science, you are not safe in history."

And this echo from the 2017 and 2018 Poet Laureate of the USA, Natasha Trethewey: "Both my parents knew that I would need an 'education by poetry' …. The role of metaphor is not only to describe our experience of reality; metaphor also shapes how we perceive reality."

Leland James
Lake Bellaire, Michigan
November, 2018

"But all the fun's in how you say a thing."

—Robert Frost, "The Mountain"

The
LITTLE RED BOOK
OF WORDPLAY:
—WITH *PERSPICACIOUS* THE CAT

tongue twister: *Six swift swordfish*
homophone: lone, loan, alone.
onomatopoeia: Biff, bap, bop
alliteration: Ten trotting turkeys ....
rhyme: rain/Jane, rain/range
simile: <u>like</u> kittens lapping
metaphor: Wild Bill is a cyclone
image: razor-like claws
personification: "Juliet is the sun."
hyperbole: he's a giant, ten feet tall
idiom: barking up the wrong tree
cliché: ~~Happy as a pig in mud.~~
        happy as bears in a bee hive
euphony: every word is a bell

" ... *all the fun's in how you say a thing.*"

INTRODUCTION
W O R D P L A Y

Wordplay is not like building with blocks,
more like hopscotch, or the tying of knots;
Or filling your pockets with exquisite rocks;
Or guessing how many a beetle has spots.

Perspicacious the cat invites you to come in
 to a wide world of words, feathered like birds
  —words that purr like a kitten
                and howl like the wind.
A fine feast, a fair frolic, a festival of words!

Vocabulary

exquisite [ik-**skwiz**-it]:
a specially high level of beauty
The pearl necklace is exquisite.

perspicacious [pur-spi-**kay** shuh s]:
keen mental ability, brainy
The perspicacious girl solved the mystery.

frolic [**frol**-ik]:
playful behavior, merriment
The children's game was a frolic.

fair [fair]:
pleasing, good
The day was fair, bright, and warm.

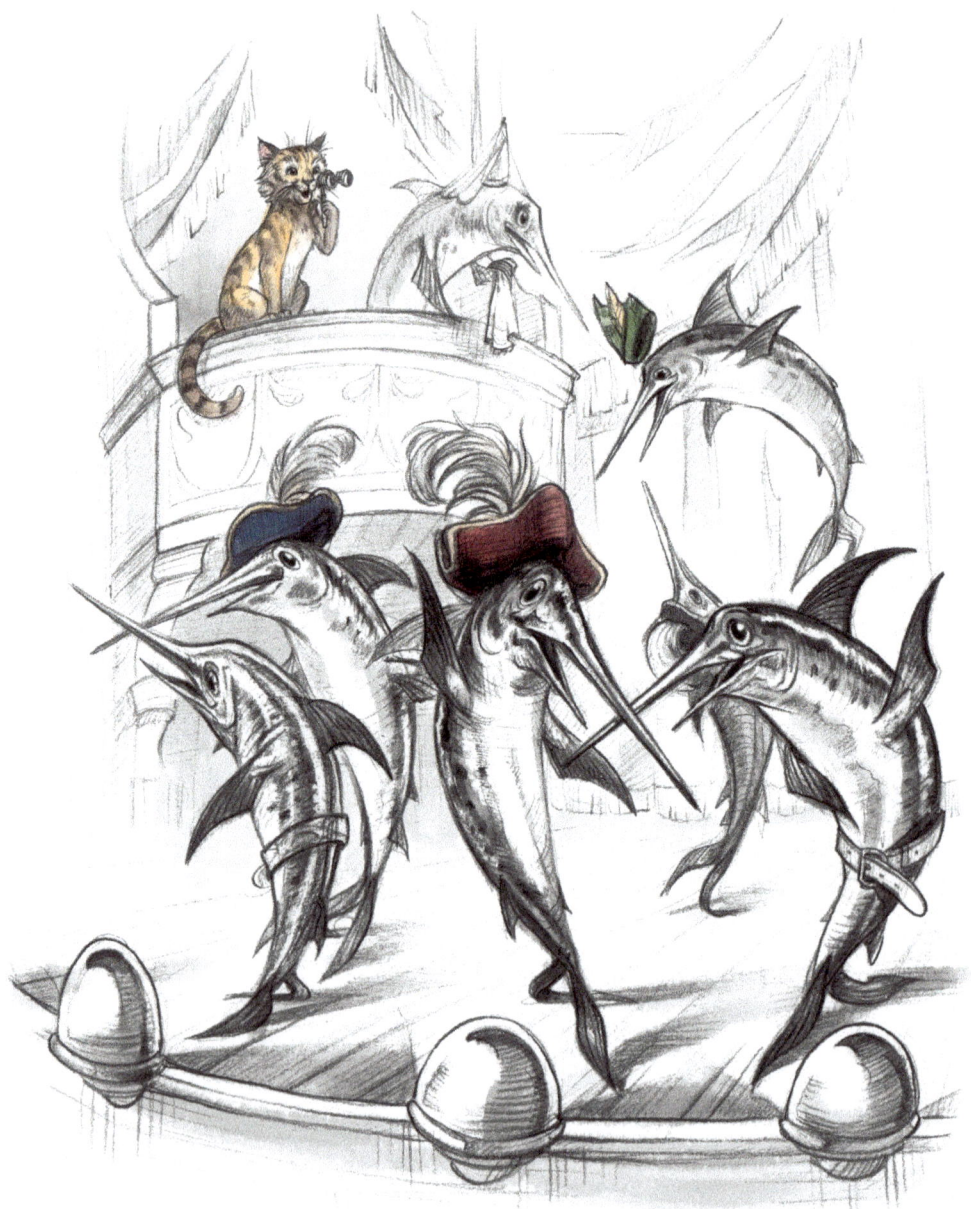

ONE
T O N G U E T W I S T E R

Tongue Twister:
a string of words difficult to pronounce

"A proper cup of coffee
from a proper copper coffee pot."

Vocabulary

audacious [aw-**day**-shuh s]:
bold, daring, lively
She is audacious, not afraid of risks.

capricious [kuh-**prish**-shuh s]:
fanciful, unpredictable
He was capricious, full of hijinks.

outlandish [out-**lan**-dish]:
purposely strange, odd
The clowns costume was outlandish.

Tongue Twister:
a string of words difficult to pronounce.

Perspicacious the cat is outspoken, audacious,
a word-music master, a caster of spells.
The cat is a rascal, capricious, outrageous:
twisting the tongue like the swirls in seashells.

He bats words about, turns them inside & ouches!
arranging word-swerving *tongue-twister* bouquets:
Six swift swordfish swordfight with their snoutses.
Six swashbuckling swordfish! Outlandish wordplays!

<u>Vocabulary</u>

audacious [aw-**day**-shuh s]:
bold, daring, lively

capricious [kuh-**prish**-shuh s]:
fanciful, unpredictable

outlandish [out-**lan**-dish]:
purposely strange, odd

Tongue Twister (continued)

<u>Definition:</u>
Tongue twister: a series of words, making sense (or seeming to) that are difficult to pronounce, especially when said quickly. (Becoming skillful in saying tongue twisters helps in better pronouncing difficult words or word sequences.) Some examples follow:

➤ **Mr. Tongue Twister tried on Tuesday to train his tongue to say twelve "Ts."**

➤ **Elizabeth Bennett's birthday is on the thirty-third Thursday.**

➤ **How much pink could a pink pinch pinch if a pink pinch could pinch pink. A pink pinch would pinch all the pink it could pinch if a pink pinch could pinch pink.**

➤ **Two witches watch one hundred and one wonderful watches.**

➤ **When a doctor doctors a doctor, does the doctor doing the doctoring doctor as the doctor being doctored wants to be doctored or does the doctor doing the doctoring doctor as he wants to doctor?**

Tongue Twister (continued)

Perspicacious challenge:
Arrange the lines below into tongue twisters by sorting the words into tongue-twisting strings that make at least some sense. Each line of words gets a little more difficult. See if you can solve all three.

Example: **lizards Lazy Lillian little on lie lets lily pads lavender**

Answer: Lazy Lillian lets little lizards lie on lavender lily pads

Six slid slippery seaward slowly snails
Answer: _____

Crisp and crunch crackle crusts
Answer: _____

fishes Five frantic from frogs fled fierce fifty
Answer: _____

TWO
H O M O P H O N E

Homophone [**hom**-uh-fohn]:
words sounding alike with different meanings

"I'm going *to* the store to buy *two* apples.
You come *too.*"

Vocabulary

caution [**kaw**-shuh n]:
a warning, or to be careful
<u>*"Look both ways"* is a caution.</u>

lone, alone, loan:
only one, to be alone, to lend,
The *lone* fisherman, *alone* in a storm,
<u>asked another fisherman to *loan* him a hand.</u>

blue, blues, the blues:
a color, a form of music, being sad
The *blue* of the autumn sky and
<u>*blues* music, made the girl feel *blue.*</u>

Homophone [**hom**-*uh*-fohn]:
words sounding alike with different meanings

A *Perspicacious*-the-cat caution:
Words may mean *this* (or *this* and that).
Multiple meanings, every so often:
lone, loan, alone; bat, bat, at the *bat.*

Owls say *"Hoo,"* not *who* or *whose.*
      Boo! and *boo-hoo.*
             Blue, blue, and the *blues.*

Words can be *mean* or *mean* many things.
A *tale* can be told and a *tail* can have rings.

Vocabulary

caution [**kaw**-shuh n]:
a warning, or to be careful

lone, alone, loan:
only one, to be alone, to lend

Blue, blues, the blues:
color, a form of music, being sad

Homophone (continued)

Definition:
Homophone [**hom**-*uh*-fohn]: two or more words pronounced the same but having different meanings, spelled the same or differently.

Bat, bat, at the *bat.* Below are many meanings:

1. a bat: a baseball bat.
2. to be at bat: standing at home plate.
3. to bat: striking at something.
4. bat: the flying mammal that lives in caves.
5. bats in the belfry: mentally unbalanced.
6. batty: also meaning mentally unbalanced.
7. Batman: the caped crusader.
8. right off the bat: right away.

Perspicacious challenge:
Find 16 homophones below. The first two are done for you.

A pair of pears is not enough for four.　　(4)

"Aye, Aye," said the first mate.
"I shall keep a watchful eye."　　(3)

I gained weight, I didn't wait.
I ate enough for six or eight!　　(　)

Knights don't fight at night. The site
where they fight is out of sight.　　(　)

If I were to be a bee, I would eat honey.　　(　)

THREE
ONOMATOPOEIA

Onomatopoeia [on-uh-mat-uh-**pee**-uh]:
words sounding like what they mean

"The **buzzing** of the bees …."

Vocabulary

drawl [drawl]:
to speak in a slow manner, stressing vowels
<u>He spoke slowly with a southern drawl.</u>

vowels [**vou**-uh l s]:
a, e, i, o, u—and *w* and *y* when they make
<u>a vowel sound</u>

verve [vurv]:
liveliness, high spirits
<u>She danced the tango with great verve.</u>

Onomatopoeia [on-uh-mat-uh-**pee**-uh]:
words sounding like what they mean

Perspicacious now sharpens his claws,
with words that mean how they sound:
Tick-tock, flip flop, ding-dong, and *draaawl.*
Whisk, wallop, wham! Hoot, holler, houund.

Biff, bop, zip-zap! Frilly, foam, fizzes.
Smash, Crash, Pow! Popcorn, ping-pong.
Stretched & stressed vowels, *z's* and *s's.*
Words with verve: *snap*-happy word songs.

Vocabulary

drawl [drawl]:
to speak in a slow manner, stressing vowels

vowels [**vou**-uh l s]:
a, e, i, o, u—and w and y when they make a
vowel sound

verve [vurv]:
liveliness, high spirits

Onomatopoeia (continued)

<u>Definitions:</u>
Vowels [**vou**-uh l s]:
a, e, i, o, u—and w and y when they make an a, e, i, o, or u sound.

Onomatopoeia [on-uh-mat-uh-**pee**-uh]: words that imitate sounds associated with the objects or actions they refer to. Note that many onomatopoeias include, and stress, vowels and/or z's and/or s's. The words in italics on the previous page are examples. Below are additional examples.

Purr: Contented cats *purr.*
Meow: The cat *meowed* to be fed.
Scratch: The cat *scratched* at the door.

Here are examples of onomatopoeias in literature and from song lyrics:

"The <u>moan</u> of doves ...."
—Alfred Lord Tennyson

"I hear the lake water <u>lapping</u> with low sounds by the shore."
—William Butler Yeats

"It went <u>zip</u> when it moved and <u>bop</u> when it stopped/And <u>whirr</u> when it stood still."
—Tom Paxton ("The Marvelous Toy")

Onomatopoeia (continued)

Perspicacious challenge:
Below is a "nonsense poem" made of onomatopoeias. Read the lines out loud, finding a rhythm. Try to make up your own nonsense poem. Use onomatopoeias from any of the previous examples. Or add your own. Arrange the words you choose into lines until you like the rhythm and sound.

Onomatopoeia Soup

bump, thump, bonk, honk, bop
achoo, moo, giggle-gurgle, plop
clip-clop, clip-clop, clip-clop
sizzle, whoop, swish, fizzle, flop

Presenting
The Onomatopoeia Trio
Meow, bow-bow, meow, bow-wow, meowww, oink-oink, bow-wowwww!
Oink, Oink, meow.
Oink, Oink, bow-wow.
Meow, Oink, Oink
bow-wowwwwwwwww!"

FOUR
ALLITERATION

Alliteration [uh-lit-uh-**rey**-shuh n]:
a string of words repeating the same sound

"Ten turkeys trotting ...."

Vocabulary

trippingly [**trip**-ing-lee]:
to move with a light, quick step
He stepped trippingly down the walk.

Dalmatian [dal-**mey**-shuh n]:
a type of dog, white with black spots
The Dalmatian is a spotted dog.

Alliteration [uh-lit-uh-**rey**-shuh n]:
a string of words repeating the same sound

Merry your words, *make* them *march* to one sound,
words *jiggling* and *juggling, skipping* like *stones,*
like *steeds spinning* around on a merry-go-*round,*
words *trippingly teasing, dancing* on your *tongue.*

— *Dalmatian dogs* are *done* up in *dark dots.*
— *Jackko juggled jack* o'lanterns in the *gym.*
—*Tongue Twisters tied* in *terribly tough* knots.
—*Teresa* and *Theodore took tomatoes to Tim.*

Vocabulary

trippingly [**trip**-ing-lee]:
to move with a light, quick step

Dalmatian [dal-**mey**-shuh n]:
a type of dog, white with black spots

Alliteration (continued)

Definition:
Alliteration [uh-lit-uh-**rey**-shuh n]: two or more words in a row that make the same sound, not always one after the other but fairly close together. Note: it is the repetition of a <u>sound</u> not necessarily a letter that makes alliteration.

Organizations use alliteration in their names:
Krispy Kreme, Coca Cola, Dunkin' Donuts, Bed, Bath & Beyond, Best Buy ….

Cartoon characters names are often alliterations:
Road Runner, Mickey Mouse, Bugs Bunny, Fred Flintstone, Daffy Duck, Porky Pig ….

Names of sports teams are often alliterations:
Buffalo Bills, Boston Bruins, Miami Marlins, Pittsburg Pirates, San Antonio Spurs ….

Candy names are often alliterations:
Bon Bons, Peppermint Patty, Tic Tacs, Jujubes, M&Ms, candy canes ….

Alliteration (continued)

Perspicacious challenge:

Here are three examples of alliteration from literature and song lyrics. Find and note the alliterations. Lines may have more than one, and the words making the alliteration are not always close together. Remember, it is the same sound not always the same letter that makes the alliteration. Ask your ear, not your eye, to find them. There are 22. The first is done for you.

"Once upon a midnight dreary <u>while</u> I
pondered <u>weak</u> and <u>weary</u>"   (3)
—Edgar Allen Poe

"The fair breeze blew, the white
foam flew"   ( )
—Samuel Taylor Coleridge

"Many mumbling mice are making
midnight music in the moonlight"   ( )
—Dr. Seuss

"I have looked down the saddest city lane"
(2 alliterations, listen closely)   ( )
—Robert Frost

"Whisper words of wisdom"   ( )
—The Beatles

midnight

mice

making

saddest

mumbling

looked

city

breeze

music

blew

land

flew

fair

foam

FIVE
PERFECT AND IMPERFECT RHYME

Perfect and Imperfect Rhyme:
words sounding alike

Perfect Rhyme: rain/chain
Imperfect Rhyme: rain/game

Vocabulary

sublime [s*uh*-**blahym**]:
exceptional, wonderful
The chocolate cake was sublime.

precocious [pri-**koh**-sh*uh* s]:
high level mental ability, advanced skill
The chess champion was precocious.

atrocious [*uh*-**troh**-sh*uh* s]:
shockingly bad, awful
The performance was atrocious!

visage [viz-ij]:
facial expression or appearance
His visage was a constant frown.

supercalifragilisticexpialidocious
[soo-per-kal-*uh*-fraj-*uh*-lis-tik-ek-spee-al-i-**doh**-sh*uh* s]:
incredibly wonderful—from the Disney movie *Mary Poppins*

Perfect/Imperfect Rhyme:
words sounding alike

Perspicacious shares the secret of rhyme:
The ear not the eye makes rhyming sublime.

Perspicacious rhymes *purrrfectly*
with *audacious.* But a whisker less kind
with outrageous, which rhymes *purrrfectly*
with *contagious;* both rhyme kinds are fine.

Rhymes: squarely or squirrely—
Squarely (perfect): rain, *Jane, chain, train*
Squirrely (imperfect): rain, *range, fame, game,*

A rhyme can be perspicacious, precocious,
audacious, atrocious, and just for fun:
    "supercalifragilisticexpialidocious"

Vocabulary

sublime [*suh*-**blahym**]:
exceptional, wonderful

precocious [pri-**koh**-shuh s]:
high level mental ability, advanced skill

atrocious [*uh*-**troh**-sh*uh* s]:
shockingly bad, awful

visage [**viz**-ij]:
facial expression or appearance

Perfect Rhyme (squarely), rain, chain
Perspicacious: [pur-spi-**kay**-shuh s]
Audacious: [aw-**day**-shuh s]

Imperfect Rhyme (squirrely), rain, game
Perspicacious: [pur-spi-**kay**-shuh s]
Contagious: [kuh n-**tay**-juh s]

Perfect/Imperfect Rhyme (continued)

Definitions:
Perfect rhyme (squarely): the final stressed syllable in two or more words rhyme, plus any (if any) unstressed syllables that follow.

Imperfect rhyme (squirrely): two or more words that sound alike. Also called near rhyme.

Perspicacious challenge:
Guess the poet's rhyme and fill in the blanks.

"Singing he was, or fluting all the **day**;
He was as fresh as is the month of ___."
—Geoffrey Chaucer, "The Canterbury Tales"

"**Double, double** toil and t _ _ _ _ _ _,
Fire burn and cauldron **bubble**..."
—William Shakespeare, *Macbeth*

"I met a traveler from an antique **land,**
Who said—Two vast and trunkless legs of **stone**
Stand in the desert . . . Near them, on the _____,
                    (rhymes with **land**)
Half sunk a shattered visage lies, whose _____,
                    (imperfect rhyme with **stone**)
And wrinkled lip, and sneer of cold command,"
—Percy Bysshe Shelley, "Ozymandias"

All poems may be easily found on the internet to check your answers.

SIX
SIMILE

Simile [**sim**-*uh*-lee]:
a comparison using *like* or *as*, sometimes *than*

"He is brave **like** a lion."
"He's as brave **as** a lion."
"He's braver **than** a lion."

Vocabulary

inspired [in-**spahy***uh* **rd**]:
to have or to cause a feeling or thought
The girl was inspired to study math.

zest [**zest**]:
liveliness, energy
He approached his studies with zest.

Assyrian [uh-seer-ee-uh]:
An inhabitant of an ancient Asian empire

Fred is fast as a rabbit,
fast as greased lighting,
faster than a rocket
—like Fred is flying!

Simile [**sim**-*uh*-lee]:
a comparison using **like** or **as**, sometimes **than**

A cat-quick trick for painting pictures
with words, alive, inspired, perspicacious:
compare any pair with zest and verve,
use <u>*like*</u> or <u>*as*</u> at a crossroad of sameness:

Fred's fast <u>*as*</u> a jet, fast <u>*as*</u> greased lightning.
He runs <u>*like*</u> a rabbit, <u>*as*</u> fast <u>*as*</u> the wind.
Fred takes off <u>*like*</u> a rocket; it's <u>*like*</u> he's flying!
<u>*Like*</u> a whirlwind, Fred leaves all others behind.

Vocabulary

inspired [in-**spahy***uh* **rd**]:
to have or to cause a feeling or thought

zest [*zest*]:
liveliness, energy

Assyrian [uh-seer-ee-uh]:
an inhabitant of an ancient Asian empire

Simile (continued)

<u>Definition:</u>
Simile [**sim**-*uh*-lee]: similar characteristics of unlike things compared by using *like*, *as*, and sometimes *than*. Below are literary examples.

"The water made a sound <u>like</u> kittens lapping."
—Marjorie Kinnan Rawlings

"The Assyrian came down <u>like</u> the wolf on the fold."
—George Gordon Byron

"I wandered lonely <u>as</u> a cloud."
—William Wordsworth

"A wondrous wonder in Longberry was simmering,
a wondrous wonderment to the brim, brimmering,
a glimmer, a glow, a Jim-Jim Jiminy Cricketing,
<u>like</u> a buzzing of bees 'round her head flickering."
—Leland James

This final example is from Longberry's Leap, *published by Little Red Tree Publishing. There is a companion book to Longberry on creative writing and poetry craft, also by Leland James. Available, with* Longberry's Leap *purchase as a free download from Little Red Tree Publishing:*
www.littleredtree.com/longberrys-leap/

Simile (continued)

Perspicacious challenge:
Use *like* or *as* to compare something to a <u>day</u> and/or the <u>weather</u> by employing the five senses. Examples below:

Sight: The clouds <u>looked</u> dark *<u>as</u>* lumps of coal.

Smell: The first whiff of bad weather <u>smelled</u> *<u>like</u>* dead fish.

Sound: The thunder <u>sounded</u> *<u>like</u>* bowling balls hitting the pins.

Taste: The day <u>tasted</u> fresh, *<u>like</u>* a red, ripe raspberry.

Touch: The day <u>felt</u> full of promise, better *<u>than</u>* a new pair of running shoes.

Make up your own *similes*, comparing a day or the weather to something else with a particular *sight, smell, sound, taste, touch*, or any combination of these.

The thunderstorm sounded *like*

The day felt full of promise, better **than** a new pair of running shoes

The clouds looked dark **as** lumps of coal

SEVEN
METAPHOR

Metaphor [**met**-*uh*-fawr]:
direct comparison, something *is* (not like or as)

"He's a lion!"

Vocabulary

forthright [**fohrth**-rahyt]:
straightforward, to the point
John was forthright in his statement.

manifest [**man**-*uh*-fest]:
shown plainly, openly
Honesty was manifest in her explanation.

euphoria [yoo-**fohr**-ee-*uh*]:
extreme happiness
He felt euphoria when he won the race.

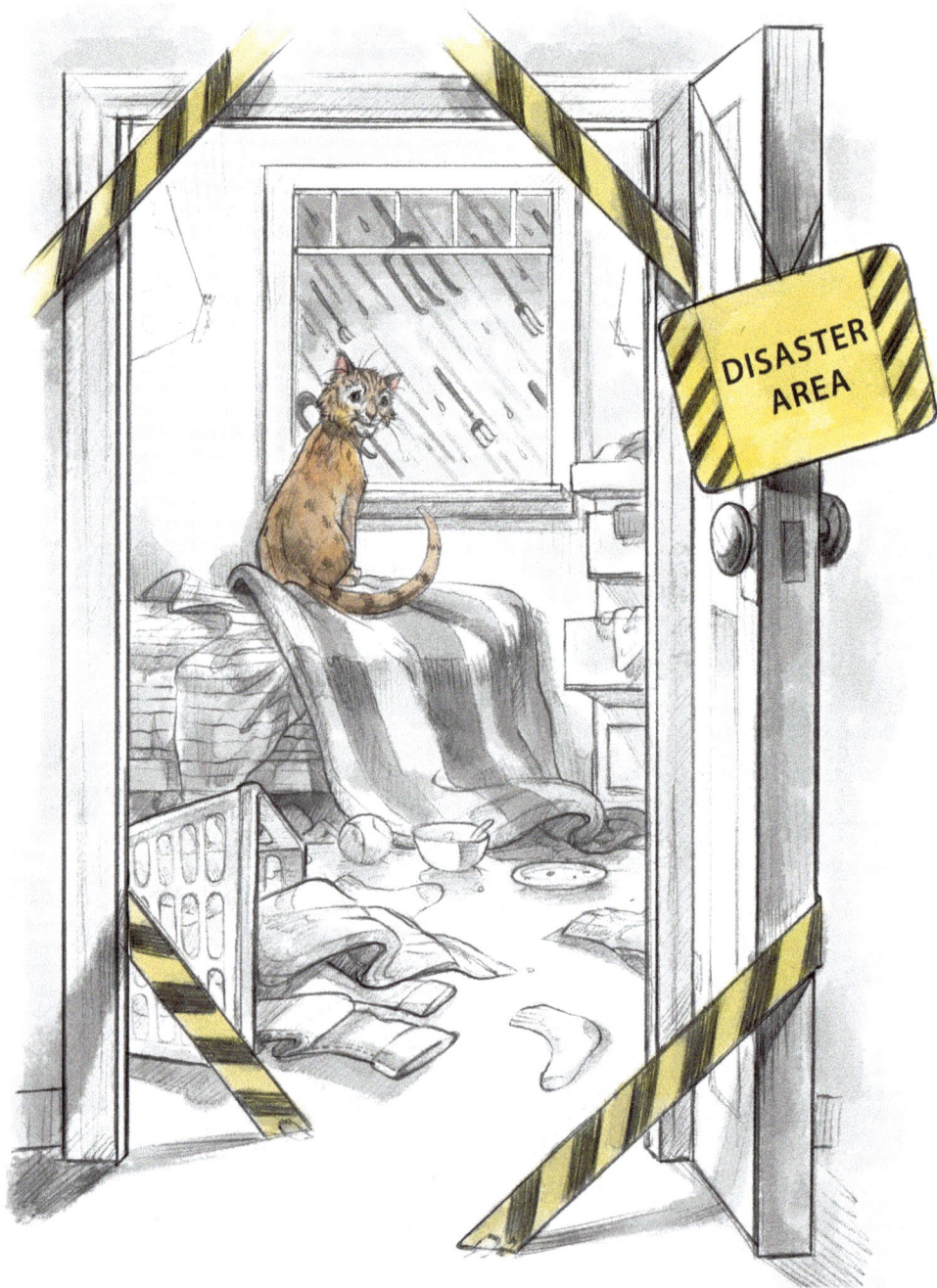

Metaphor [**met**-*uh*-fawr]:
direct comparison, something *is* (not like or as)

A metaphor is (~~like/as~~) a simile at heart,
without *like* or *as,* more bold, forthright,
a comparison direct, without the spare part,
a comparison daring, manifest, watertight:

> Fast Fred *is ~~like~~* a rabbit.
> Fast Fred *is ~~as fast as~~* a rabbit.

Do you sometimes feel *down* when it rains
pitchforks? Is your room a *disaster area?*
Are the math problems *rattling* your brain?
Did the flowers bloom in a burst of *euphoria?*

Vocabulary

forthright [**fohrth**-rahyt]:
straightforward, to the point

manifest [**man**-*uh*-fest]:
shown plainly, openly

euphoria [yoo-**fohr**-ee-*uh*]:
extreme happiness

Metaphor (continued)

Definition:

Metaphor [**met**-*uh*-fawr]: similar characteristics of persons, things, or ideas *compared* by direct reference (without *like* or *as*). Examples below.

"Juliet is the sun."
—William Shakespeare

"'Hope' is the thing with feathers."
—Emily Dickinson

"Life for me ain't been no crystal stair.
It's had tacks in it,
And splinters."
—Langston Hughes

"Mr. Grinch. You're a bad banana with a greasy black peel."
—Dr. Seuss

"A wondrous wonder in Longberry was simmering,
a wondrous wonderment to the brim, brimmering,
a glimmer, a glow, a Jim-Jim Jiminy Cricketing,
like a buzzing of bees 'round her head flickering."
—Leland James

Note that this example from a previous page has a simile (like) in the final line. Each of the first three lines is a metaphor, Longberry's wonder:... simmering ... brimmering ... Jiminy Cricketing.

Metaphor (continued)

Perspicacious challenge:
Pick several persons you know, or characters from books, and think of metaphors that describe the person or some part of their personality. Here are examples.

Wild Bill is a <u>cyclone.</u>

The detective, Sherlock Holmes, is a <u>fox.</u>

Trustworthy Tom is a <u>rock</u> of integrity.

Betty is a <u>blooming rose.</u>

Bob is a <u>busy bee.</u>

Perspicacious is a <u>magician</u> with words.

Character _____:

He or She is a/an _____.

EIGHT
I M A G E

Image [**im**-ij]:
a word picture painted with words
in one or more of the five senses

"The sun rose like a golden coin."

Vocabulary

essence [**es**-*uh* ns]:
basic nature, most important
<u>The essence of a flower is its beauty.</u>

endeavor [en-**dev**-er]:
to try, to make an effort
<u>Defending her friend was a brave endeavor.</u>

adjectives [**aj**-ik-tiv s]:
words that *describe* other words
The **big brown grizzly** bear ....
The three words in bold, above,
<u>*describe* a bear—they are "adjectives."</u>

Image [**im**-ij]:
a *word picture* painted with words in one or more
of the five senses

Simile and Metaphor, in essence a pair—
Two brothers who ever endeavor the same:
to *compare*. Word *pictures*, out of thin air:
to *persuade*, to *inform* or *entertain*.

Not just a *big brown grizzly* bear.
Such *description* is fine, as far as it goes.
But what makes this bear really rare?
Compare! Give the bear a *clown's* nose.

Or with Compare, make a scary bear:
A bear *tall as a tree* with *razor-like* claws.
Give him eyes *like a demon*, put *fire* in his glare.
Leaves *grow pale* at this grizzly's growls.
He's a *monster*, a *devil*—beware of this bear!

Vocabulary

essence [**es**-*uh* ns]:
basic nature, most important

endeavor [en-**dev**-er]:
to try, to make an effort

adjectives [**aj**-ik-tiv s]:
words that describe other words

Image (continued)

Definition:
Image [**im**-ij]: a representation (word picture) of something or someone. Images call to mind mental pictures based on sight, smell, taste, sound, and touch. Below are examples of similes and metaphors employing each of the five senses:

Metaphors, sight:
She <u>has cherry-red</u> hair and <u>sky-blue</u> eyes.

Simile, smell:
Ma's kitchen <u>smelled like Christmas.</u>

Metaphor, taste:
He was a <u>pickle-mouthed</u> old man.

Metaphor, sound:
We heard the <u>tin-can rattle</u> of the old Ford truck.

Simile, touch:
The wind on the beach was <u>rough as sandpaper</u>.

Image (continued)

Perspicacious challenge:

Fill in the blanks with a word or phrase from the choices in bold below, turning each sentence into a metaphor or a simile. Make each an *image* that makes sense.

She has an _____ of children.
     (metaphor)

Her eyes were a _____ gray.
     (metaphor)

John climbs like a _____.
     (simile)

He's strong as an _____.
     (simile)

That old computer is a _____.
     (metaphor)

ox   army   dinosaur   monkey   stormy

NINE
PERSONIFICATION

Personification [per-son-uh-fi-**kay**-shuh n]:
giving human qualities to animals or things

"The tree waved its branches
like a Halloween witch."

Vocabulary

devise [dih-**vahyz**]:
to create from available parts
We will devise a plan to build a tree house.

scold [skohld]:
to find fault, criticize
Mother will scold me for being late.

Personification
[per-son-uh-fi-kay-shuh n]:
giving human qualities to
animals or things.

Personification [per-son-uh-fi-**kay**-shuh n]:
giving human qualities to animals or things

Metaphor has a sister as well as a brother—
To the family Compare, add *Personification.*
She works with her brothers, one or the other.
With her help they devise *fantastic* creations:

Dawn, with a *kiss, wakes up Old Man River.*
Animals *talk*: chipmunks *scold*, owls *advise.*
A blackberry bush in the winter wind *shivers.*
Each day is *born* and each night the day *dies.*

Vocabulary

devise [dih-**vahyz**]:
to create from available parts

scold [skohld]:
to find fault, criticize

Personification (continued)

Definition:

Personification [per-son-uh-fi-**kay**-shuh n]: a comparison in which an animal, thing, or idea is given human qualities, or sometimes nonliving things are given animal qualities. (*Perspicacious* the cat is a personification of the word *perspicacious*.) Personification can occur in either a metaphor or a simile. *Personification* is a broad category of which there are subcategories. These may be saved for a later time. The following examples from literature are personifications that are metaphors. They do not employ *like* or *as*.

"[T]he boy came back and the tree shook with joy."
—Shel Silverstein

"April is the cruellest month,"
—T.S. Eliot

"The fog comes/on little cat feet."
— Carl Sandburg

"The tall dog purrs at the purple moon.
The silver bee stings the red balloon.
The tall dog laughs to see such fun,
and the moon eats the stars with a spoon."
—Leland James

"Have you got a brook in your little heart,"
—Emily Dickinson

Personification (continued)

Perspicacious challenge:
Create a personification for an animal or a thing creating a particular mood.

Examples:

Fear: The leaves *shook with fear.*
—*metaphor/personification*

Joy: The sun was smiling *like it knew* it was my birthday.
—*metaphor/simile/personification*

Anger: The rattlesnake took *revenge* on the hiker who disturbed its nest.
–*metaphor/personification*

Sadness: The day *rained tears* on the *grieving city.*
—*metaphors/personifications*

Good fortune: As if he'd won the lottery, the squirrel eyed the bowl of nuts.
—*simile/personification*

For each of the above moods, fear, joy, anger, sadness, and having good fortune, create a personification in a metaphor or a simile.

TEN
H Y P E R B O L E

Hyperbole [hahy-**pur**-buh-lee]:
extreme exaggeration

"The lumberjack had
the strength of ten men!"

Vocabulary

brash [brash]:
energetic, loud, outspoken
The car salesman was brash.

dramatization [dram-uh-tuh-**zey**-shuh n]:
to expresses as if in a drama
The story was a dramatization of events.

crow [kroh]:
to boast or cry out with pleasure
He crowed about his victory.

prevarication [pri-var-i-**key**-shuh n]:
lying, untruth
His explanation was a prevarication.

World's Smartest
Animal!
(Brave and kind too)

Hyperbole [hahy-**pur**-b*uh*-lee]:
extreme exaggeration

Now, Metaphor's brash, big-city cousin:
a flashy fellow of the family Compare,
boastful, a showoff: brags by the dozen,
a barnful of crows, balloons of *hot air.*

Exaggeration's his game: *He's a giant, ten feet tall!*
                —such dramatization!—
and he's smart *as a whip* and as *wise as an owl.*

It's just good fun, just *fish-story* whales.
It's not prevarication—it's just tall tales.

Vocabulary

brash [brash]:
energetic, loud, outspoken

dramatization [dram-uh-tuh-**zey**-shuh n]:
to expresses as if in a drama

crow [kroh]:
to boast or cry out with pleasure

prevarication [pri-var-i-**key**-shuh n]:
lying, untruth

Hyperbole (continued)

Definition:
Hyperbole [hahy-**pur**-b*uh*-lee]: the use of extreme exaggeration for the purpose of emphasis or humor, not intended to be taken as true. Below are examples from literature:

"Why does a boy who's fast <u>as</u> a jet take all day and sometimes two to get to school?"
—John Ciadri (simile/hyperbole)

"I'll love you, dear, I'll love you
Till China and Africa meet,
And the river jumps over the mountain
And the salmon sing in the street,"
—W.H. Auden (metaphors/hyperbole)

"I got a dog, he's mighty fine.
Brushes his teeth with turpentine.
This dog of mine, he's one fine gent,
Think I'll run him for president."
—Leland James (metaphors/hyperbole)

Hyperbole (continued)

Perspicacious challenge:
Create a comparison using hyperbole for a characteristic of a person, animal or activity, either simile or metaphor. The final two are the higher degrees of difficulty.

Examples:

Strength: He's a bulldozer when arguing.
—metaphor/hyperbole

Sight: She has eyes like an eagle
—smile/hyperbole

Speed: He is faster than a speeding bullet.
—simile/hyperbole

Depth: It is deep as the sea.
—simile/hyperbole

Goodness: She's an angel.
—metaphor/hyperbole

ELEVEN
I D I O M

Idiom [**id**-ee-*uh* m]:
a word string with a special meaning,
outside dictionary definitions

"He's cool as a cucumber."
—calm, unrattled

Vocabulary

askew [*uh*-**skyoo**]:
out of line, topsy-turvy
The king's crown was askew.

at the drop of a hat (an idiom)
a sudden action or decision

I'm all ears (an idiom)
listening closely

at loggerheads (an idiom)
in extreme disagreement

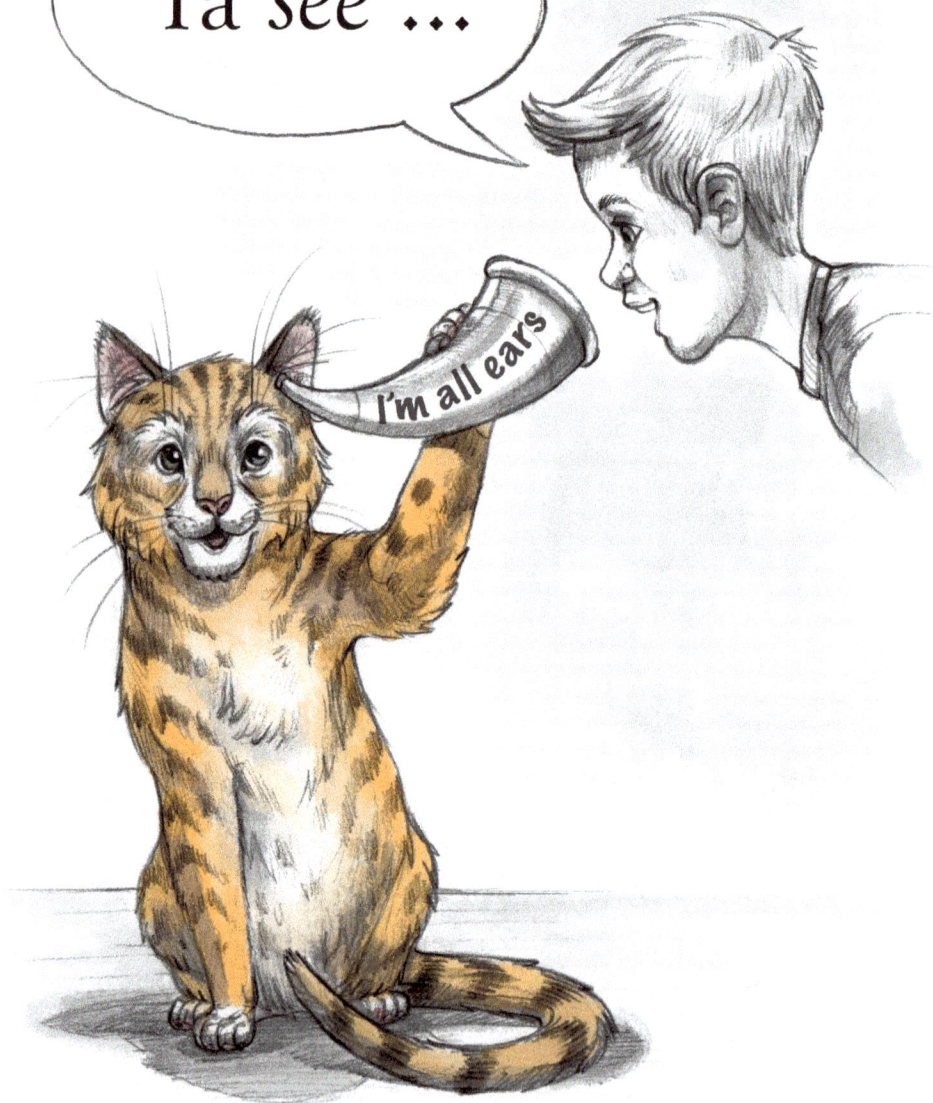

Idiom [**id**-ee-uh m]:
a word string with a special meaning,
outside dictionary definitions

Words may mean more than *this* (and that),
words *a mite strange*, meanings brand new
hat/ the/ at/ a/ of/ drop: "At the drop of a hat." But
no hat hits the ground—meanings askew.

"I'm all ears," says Bob to his friend Betty Sue.
Does Bob have no nose, no fingers or toes?
Is he really *all ears*? No. Bob has just two.
Everyone knows: ears come in pairs, not rows.

So Ya-*see* (*listen up!*): You need to be wary.
              Words may be at *loggerheads*
                          with the dictionary.

Vocabulary

askew [*uh*-**skyoo**]:
out of line, topsy-turvy

at the drop of a hat (an idiom)
a sudden action or decision

I'm all ears (an idiom)
listening closely

at loggerheads (an idiom)
in extreme disagreement

Idiom (continued)

Definition:
Idiom [**id**-ee-*uh* m]: an expression, often a metaphor, whose meaning is not predictable from the dictionary definitions of the words employed. Below are bits of dialogue that illustrate how the *literal* (usual) or dictionary meaning of the words assembled in an idiom may be misunderstood.

Dialogue, from *Star Trek IV The Voyage Home*, between Captain Kirk and Spock (who was not raised on earth and might not know its idioms):

Kirk: "If we *play our cards right*, we'll find out when those whales will be released."
Spock: "How will playing cards help?"
—*play our cards right:* necessary to succeed

Imagined dialogue between Kirk and Spock:

Kirk: *"A piece of cake."*
Spock: "Captain, we've no time for dessert."
—*piece of cake:* easy to accomplish

Kirk: "We're *barking up the wrong tree.*"
Spock: "Captain, we are certainly not barking!"
—*barking up the wrong tree:* looking in the wrong place

Kirk: "We need to *fish or cut bait!*"
Spock: "This is no time for fishing."
—*fish or cut bait:* pursue or stop trying

Idiom (continued)

Perspicacious challenge:
Fill in the blanks from the choices in bold below, creating idioms.

I'm feeling a bit _____.

I was able to kill _____.

We're late for the concert. We totally _____.

That argument is a _____.

That's not true. He was just _____.

**hot potato   spinning a yarn   missed the boat
two birds with one stone   under the weather**

TWELVE
CLICHÉ

Cliché [klee-**shey**]:
overused words

"She's got a bee in her bonnet."

Vocabulary

fossilization [**fos**-uh l *uh*-**zey** sh*uh* n]:
living things preserved in stone
It was so old, fossilization had set in.

recast [ree-**kast**]:
to form, fashion, or arrange anew
She decided to recast her letter to Grandma.

Happy as a kid in a candy store
~~Happy as a kid in a candy store~~
~~Happy as a pig in mud~~
~~Happy as a lark~~

Happy as the candles on a birthday cake!

Cliché [klee-**shey**]:
overused words

A *catchphrase* has *caught on*, sticks tight.
Metaphor,
        simile,
                hyperbole,
                        idiom,
                                personification:
all have *sticktights*, words old, lost their bite.
Words worn out, looking tired—*fossilization.*

With a pencil, word glue, and a tube of creation,
recast those *sticktights* with new inspiration!

Vocabulary

fossilization [**fos**-uh l *uh-zey* sh*uh* n]:
living things preserved in stone

recast [ree-**kast**]:
to form, fashion, or arrange again

Cliché (continued)

Definition:

Cliché [klee-**shey**]: an expression that has lost its impact through overuse. Clichés can be useful when speaking, as an effective way to get a point across quickly. For instance, suggesting the need for a plan of action: "Let's get our ducks in a row." They also may be used for ease of understanding in teaching—often used in this way on previous pages. But as a general rule, when writing, use clichés sparingly. Clichés, overused, can make writing *dull as dishwater.*

Below are several commonly overused clichés, all regarding time:

in the nick of time – to happen just in time
only time will tell – to become clear over time
a matter of time – to happen sooner or later
at the speed of light – done quickly
lasted an eternity – to last for a very long time
lost track of time – no attention to time

Cliché (continued)

Perspicacious challenge:
Create a substitute for the following *"clichés."*

Alternatives for this cliché: **happy as a kid in a candy store**

happy as bear in a bee hive
happy as candles on a birthday cake
happy as a cat with a rat
happy as a dog diggin' a hole
happy as the sails on a toy boat
happy as the first day of spring
happy as a skunk eatin' bumble bees

Think of alternatives for each of these clichés.

busy as a bee

clumsy as a bull in a china shop

higher than a kite

dull as dishwater

THIRTEEN
E U P H O N Y

Euphony [**yoo**-*fuh*-nee]:
a pleasing sound, particularly of words

"The field was the color of honey,
a fine sun baked brown."

Vocabulary

paramount [**par**-*uh*-mount]:
first in importance
Attendance was of paramount importance.

in concert (an idiom)
done together, jointly

tongue twister: *Six swift swordfish*
homophone: lone, loan, alone.
onomatopoeia: Biff, bap, bop
alliteration: Ten trotting turkeys ....
rhyme: *rain*/Jane, *rain*/range
simile: <u>like</u> kittens lapping
metaphor: Wild Bill is a cyclone
image: razor-like claws
personification: "Juliet is the sun."
hyperbole: he's a giant, ten feet tall
idiom: barking up the wrong tree
cliché: ~~Happy as a pig in mud.~~
         happy as bears in a bee hive
euphony: every word is a bell

" *... all the fun's in how you say a thing.*"

Euphony [**yoo**-*fuh*-nee]:
a pleasing sound, particularly of words

Perspicacious the cat says, "Mark this well!
Listen close, make this paramount in your mind:
Each word has its sound, every word is a bell,
in concert a voice; *listen close* and you'll find
words thunder and wimper, whisper and tell….
Words play together, whoop, wonder, and sing!
And " … all the fun's in how you say a thing."

Robert Frost, former Poet Laureate of the USA wrote
this:

"… warm/Compared with cold, and cold compared
with warm./But all the fun's in how you say a thing."
—from "The Mountain"

Vocabulary

paramount [**par**-*uh*-mount]:
first in importance

in concert (an idiom)
done together, jointly

Euphony (continued)

Definition:
Euphony [**yoo**-*fuh*-nee]: a pleasing sound, particularly a harmonious string of words.

Perspicacious challenge:
See if you can think of an example for all of the following terms. Try to make your examples have euphony.

tongue twister: a string of words difficult to pronounce.
homophone[**hom**-*uh*-fohn]: words sounding alike with different meanings.
onomatopoeia [on-*uh*-mat-*uh*-**pee**-*uh*]: words sounding like what they mean.
alliteration [*uh*-lit-*uh*-**rey**-sh*uh* n]: a string of words repeating the same sound.
rhyme: [rahym]: words sounding alike.
simile [**sim**-*uh*-lee]: a comparison using *like* or *as*, sometimes *than*.
metaphor [**met**-*uh*-fawr]: direct comparison, something is (not like or as).
image [im-ij]: a word picture painted in one or more of the five senses.
personification [per-son-*uh*-fi-**kay**-sh*uh* n]: giving human qualities to animals or things.
hyperbole [hahy-**pur**-b*uh*-lee]: extreme exaggeration.
idiom [**id**-ee-*uh* m]: a word string with a special meaning, outside dictionary definitions.
cliché [klee-**shey**]: overused words.
euphony [**yoo**-*fuh*-nee]: a pleasing sound, particularly of words.

ABOUT THE ILLUSTRATOR

Anne Zimanski

Anne is an freelance artist, who was proudly born and raised in Southeast Michigan, and is a published children's book illustrator. She has a BFA in Illustration from Kendall College of Art and Design with a strong background in both fine art and digital illustration. Anne is a very versatile artist, experienced in a wide range of styles and media.

Anne has been a volunteer with local non-profit art groups for over 10 years, in her hometown of Milford, MI. From a young age she has worked on fund-raisers and has entered many art shows, frequently winning top awards and honorable mentions.

Visit her website to see more of her work and for more information: www.annezimanski.com

ABOUT THE AUTHOR

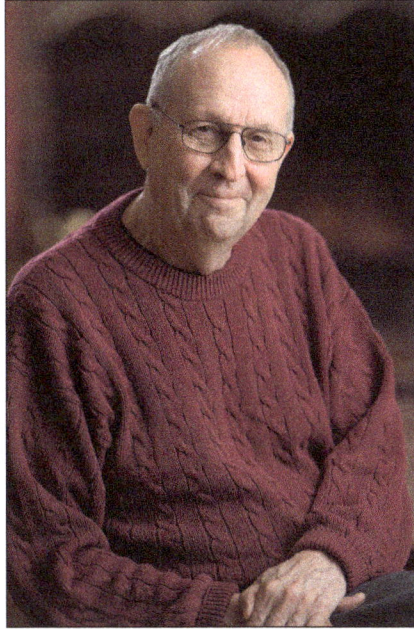

Leland James

Leland James is the author of four books poetry, three children's books in verse, and two books on creative writing and poetry craft. He has published more than 200 poems in poetry venues worldwide, including: *Rattle, The Lyric, Form Quarterly, HQ, The Haiku Quarterly, The South Carolina Review, Spoon River Poetry Review, New Millennium Writings, London Magazine, The London Reader, The American Cowboy, Ruminate, Nomos, The Delinquent, and Taj Mahal Review*. He was winner of the UK's *Aesthetica Magazine* Creative Writing Award for Poetry, The Little Red Tree International Poetry Prize, the *Portland Pen* Poetry Prize, the *Writer's Forum* short poem contest, a winner of an *Atlanta Review* International Publication Prize, and received the Franklin-Christoph Merit

Award for Poetry. He was runners-up for the poetry prizes of the *Sequestrum* Editor's Reprint Awards, the Fish International Prize in Ireland, the Welsh International, *The London Magazine*, and *Writer's Digest*. He has received honors in dozens of other competitions, including the Golden Quill Awards, the Bridport Prize, Morton Marr, *The Southwest Review*. Leland has been featured in Ted Koozer's *American Life in Poetry* and was recently nominated for a Push Cart Prize. www.lelandjamespoet.com.

Leland lives and writes in a cabin in the woods in northern Michigan. He cuts his own firewood and shovels a couple hundred inches of snow each year. Delivering readings of his own and other's poetry, he travels widely to libraries and schools. He is an outspoken proponent of meter, rhyme, and accessibility in poetry, as well as endorsing experimental and "free verse."

www.ingramcontent.com/pod-product-compliance
Lightning Source LLC
Chambersburg PA
CBHW060900090426
42738CB00022B/3480